Reptiles and Amphibians

GREAT STORY & COOL FACTS

Introduction

Welcome to Half and Half books, a great combination of story and facts! You might want to read this book on your own. However, the section with real facts is a little more difficult to read than the story. You might find it helpful to read the facts section with your parent, or someone else, who can help you with the more difficult words. Your parent may also be able to answer any questions you have about the facts—or at least help you find more information!

Reptiles and Amphibians

English Edition Copyright © 2009 by Treasure Bay, Inc.
English Edition translated by Elizabeth Bell and edited by Sindy McKay
Original edition Copyright © Nathan/VUEF 2002, Paris, France.
Original Edition: Reptiles et amphibiens

Special thanks to Ned McAllister, herpetologist, for his advice and review
of the information in this book.

The Call of the Sea by Christophe Lambert, illustrations by Gaëtan Dorémus

Non-fiction text by Jane Hervé, illustrations by Yves Beaujard, Marc Lizano,
Nathalie Lacoste, Olivier Nadel, Jean-Marie Poissenot, Michaël Welpy.
Cartoon spot illustrations by Bruno Salamone.

Anecdotes and test by Benoît Dahan. Activity by Sabine Lamy,
with illustrations by Bruno Salamone and photographs by Frédéric Hanoteau.
Puzzle game by Daniel Guerrier.

Photography Credits
Sunset/FLPA; Jacana/Photo Researchers/D. M. Schleser;
Hemera Technologies Inc. (© 1997-2001); Bios/M. Gunther;
Soug Perrine/Seapics/Joël Halioua Editorial Agency; and Jacana/Ingo Arndt.

Published by Treasure Bay, Inc.
P.O. Box 119, Novato, CA 94948 USA

PRINTED IN SINGAPORE

Library of Congress Catalog Card Number: 2008932257

ISBN: 978-1-60115-214-5

Visit us online at:
www.HalfAndHalfBooks.com

PR 11-14

Reptiles and Amphibians

Table of Contents

Facts: Yikes! Frogs, Crocodiles, Snakes and More!

The Call of the Sea

Story by **Christophe Lambert**
Illustrated by **Gaëtan Dorémus**

In the beginning . . .

I open my eyes for the first time and there, far above me, is the black sky studded with stars. I need to move up toward the stars and out to the surf that I hear crashing in the distance. How do I know this? I'm not sure exactly . . . It's as if all the experience of earlier generations of turtles is packed inside my head, like air in a balloon. The balloon pops, and thousands of tiny nuggets of knowledge shower my brain.

I guess this is what is called "instinct."

All around me, other eggs are hatching. Shells crack and split, revealing the tooth-like horn at the tip of each baby's snout. My nest-mates and I climb on top of one another. There are dozens and dozens of us and we all have the same goal: survival.

I am a sea turtle; a hawksbill turtle, to be precise. I have just been born this very moment.

I will never know my mother. She laid her eggs on this beach last spring, and it is now early autumn. She dug a deep hole in the sand in which to lay over 100 eggs, then camouflaged the nest well, using twigs, branches, and sand. This helped to hide the eggs from the badgers, foxes, and weasels that might have eaten all the eggs before they were hatched.

Now that I have safely emerged from my egg, I know that the most important job of my life lies before me. I must make my way out of this nest and into the open sea.

My journey begins with a struggle to climb up out of the hole where I was born. Flipper-legs, designed for swimming, not walking, scrabble on the ground and the sand. My nest-mates and I crawl over each other. It is a terrible, terrifying crush and the weakest fall back down into the deep nest to die.

With great difficulty, using my webbed claws, I pull myself up the slope. A sand-slide sends three turtles behind me back to the bottom. How many of us will make it to the sea, I wonder?

The urge to survive is powerful. It gives me the strength to keep fighting my way to the top of the nest.

Across the sand

As I near the top, the smell of the salt sea air is stronger and the sound of the waves is louder. I must reach the ocean. Though I have never seen it, I know it is where I belong. I feel it. Instinct, remember?

With a gigantic effort, I hoist myself out of the hole, and there it is before me: the vast expanse of water that draws me like a magnet. The stars and moon are reflected on its surface. Waves break and vanish on the shore with a gentle lapping motion.

It is beautiful. I can't tear my eyes away from this universe that is so new, yet strangely familiar. It seems to stretch out its arms to welcome me.

Now it is a race to the ocean, a marathon of baby turtles. Our instincts tell us we must take advantage of the cool night air. If we don't hurry, the hot sun of the day will sap our strength and we will fail in our mission to reach the sea.

Unfortunately, our flippers are made to move through water, not through sand. Our progress is slow.

Hungry Sea Birds

Suddenly, we hear a piercing cry:

"Aaaaaaahh!"

Huge sea birds are diving down on us. Death is falling from the sky!

I see the long sharp beak of one bird snap shut on the turtle beside me. He is swept off into the sky. Another bird swoops down. Then another and another!

The birds are fast, so there is no chance of running away. In fact, there is nothing I can do but hope that I will not be the next victim.

Fear spurs a new energy in me. My flippers shuffle frantically on the sand. I imagine myself in the water, free to swim. Delicious algae awaits there for me to eat. The cool salt water will soon be my home!

All around me the terrible attacks continue. Yet I understand that the sea birds are only following their instincts as well. These birds must eat. Young turtles are their food. This is Nature.

Still, *my* instinct drives me to be one who will survive.

Attack of the Crabs

I look ahead of me and see that the ocean is not far now. Perhaps I will make it after all! Three feet . . . two feet . . . one foot . . .

But wait! A horrible new danger now appears: dozens of hard-shelled creatures, armed with terrifying pincers. They run sideways, with great speed, on their many-jointed legs.

They are crabs.

The dreadful beasts spread out among us. Their pincers crush the soft shells of several tiny turtles around me.

A crab tries to block my way. I slip between its legs. Its lethal choppers clack above my head like castanets. Click-clack-click! The persistent crab lunges to the left, to the right, but I am one step ahead.

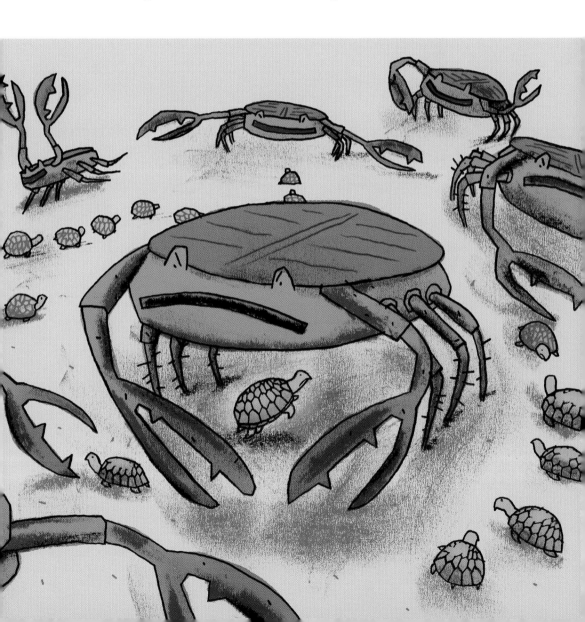

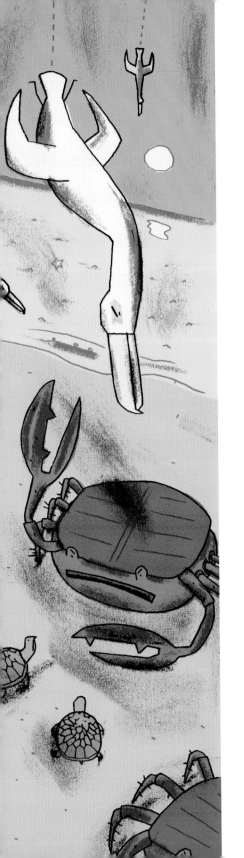

At last, my opponent gets tired of the game and goes for a different turtle unlucky enough to be passing within its reach.

I keep going without looking back. Only a few more inches and I will be safe.

Suddenly, from out of nowhere, another crab blocks my path. Its pincers are snapping, ready to destroy me.

I am paralyzed with terror, able to do nothing now but wait to be eaten.

"Aiiiiiiiiiiiiiiiiiiiiiiiiiiiiiiiiiiiiiiiii!"

A sea bird has jumped into the fray. The bird dives, beak first, onto the crab. These crabs are another favorite food of the sea birds!

Quick, Into the Water!

I dash as fast as I can into the foamy sea water that is frothing on the shore. It surrounds me, immerses me in its purity. My fear and fatigue fall away instantly in this flood of well-being.

I push off from the ground and begin floating, suddenly graceful and nimble in this new environment. My flippers begin to move, perfectly coordinated. It's as though I've been doing it all my life.

With a sense of sheer delight I realize that I have made it. I have survived!

I try to resist, but I cannot help glancing back at the shore. The sea birds and crabs are wreaking havoc on the latecomers. Sometimes two predators fight over the same prey. The birds almost always win.

A new energy fills me as I swim swiftly and skillfully toward the open sea, grateful that I have endured.

There were a little over a hundred of us in the beginning. How many of our brothers and sisters have died by now? I'd say at least seventy-five.

It is sad that so many failed, yet I know it is all part of the balance of Nature.

I look around at the others who managed to make it across the beach alive. We are the next generation of sea turtles. I think of how fortunate we are to be safe now.

I am wrong.

Suddenly a shadow slides through the water. The dark mass has jaws bristling with pointed teeth. It is a shark.

Without blinking, the huge animal swallows several of my fellow nest-mates. Again the young turtles are helpless to defend themselves. I wonder if this shark, swimming along with its mouth open, even knows that it has just gulped down these tiny creatures.

The shark passes by us and we are buffeted by the waves in its wake.

Once more I have survived the random fate of Nature, alive but in shock. Why must a young turtle's struggle for life be so harsh?

There will be more dangers I am sure, including that most dangerous predator of all—man.

But soon I will grow. My shell will become so hard that predators will break

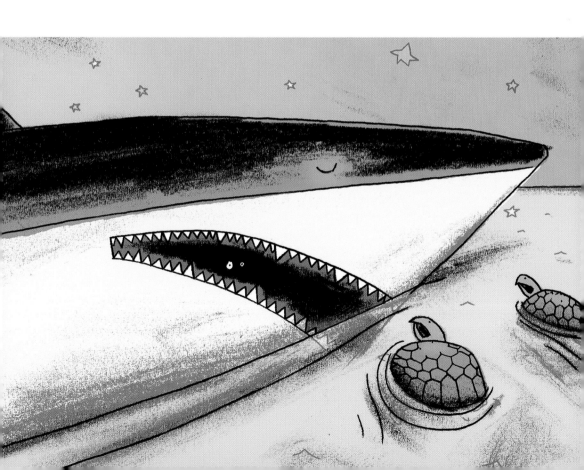

their teeth on it. Then I may survive more than a hundred years! The thought of this makes the struggle worthwhile.

After all, where there is life, there is hope.

And Life Goes On . . .

The current carries me far from the shore. I let myself be pulled along, too exhausted to resist. The water is cool and comforting and makes me feel peaceful.

Soon a golden disk appears on the horizon.

It is my first sunrise. The magnificent spectacle does my heart good. I no longer fear the sun now that I am protected by the cool ocean. My instinct tells me that it is a friend. Its rays will be absorbed by my dark shell, providing me with just the right amount of heat to help me to grow strong and to thrive.

If all goes well, I too will return to the same beach someday to lay my eggs . . . and the race for survival will begin all over again.

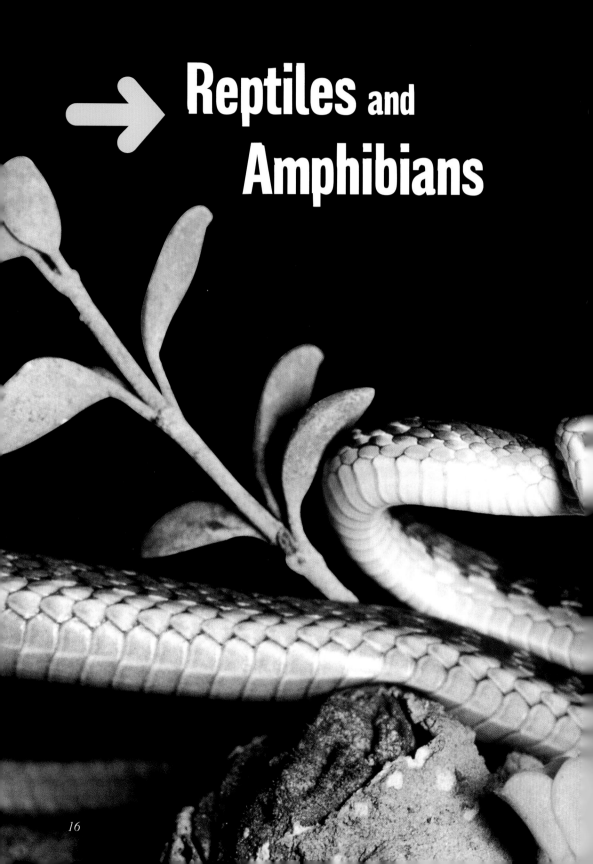

Reptiles and Amphibians

Scientists believe that *amphibians* (am fib′ē əns) were among the first animals to come on land. They evolved from fish around 400 million years ago. The first *reptiles* were descendants of amphibians. They appeared around 320 million years ago. That's about 100 million years before dinosaurs appeared. Amphibians and reptiles still thrive today, long after the extinction of dinosaurs.

There are about 12,000 species of amphibians and reptiles. All are vertebrates (vur′tə brāts), which means they have a spinal column in their back. They are also all cold-blooded, which means they must use their environment to warm or cool their bodies. The skin of most amphibians is smooth and moist, while that of reptiles is dry and covered with scales. Most amphibians lay eggs in water. Most reptiles lay eggs on land, but some reptiles develop in eggs that remain within the mother's body until they hatch. Most amphibians undergo metamorphosis (met′ə môr′fə sis), changing their form as they develop into adults. However, as reptiles grow, they shed their skin, which is called molting.

Big Families

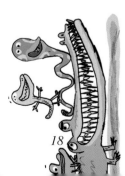

There are about 5,000 species of amphibians and 7,000 species of reptiles. They are often classified by their physical appearance, where they live, or the way they breathe, eat, or reproduce. Scientists still do not all agree on the classification and number of species in the various orders of these animals.

AMPHIBIANS

In their first stage of development, amphibian larvae *(lär´vē)* live in water, but adults live on land. They usually have two pairs of limbs. Their skin is smooth and moist, and they can breathe both through their skin and through their lungs. They may be insectivorous *(in´sek tiv´ər əs – insect eating)* or carnivorous *(kär niv´ər əs – flesh eating.)* They are divided into three ORDERS:

① **Anura – Frogs and toads** have a large head, long back legs and no tail. Their larvae are born without limbs.

Over 4,000 species

toad

frog

② **Apoda** They have no legs. They live underground.

Over 150 species

caecilian (se sil´yen)
(These are not earthworms or snakes.)

③ **Caudata or urodele** *(yoor´ə dēl´)* Salamanders and newts have an elongated body and can crawl.

About 400 species

axolotl

newt

salamander

European cave salamander

REPTILES

They evolved from amphibians, but they can crawl or slither on the ground and live in the open air. They breathe through their lungs. Their skin is dry and scaly. They are divided into 4 ORDERS:

① **Rhynchocephalia** *(rin´kō sə fā lē ən)* or Tuatara has only one species, the sphenodon (sfē´nə dän´) It is carnivorous and **oviparous** (ō vip´ər əs), which means it lays

1 species

sphenodon

② **Chelonians** (kə lō´nē əns) or *Testudines* Turtles and tortoises have bodies enclosed in a bony shell covered with scales made of horn. They live in the ocean, in rivers, and on land. They eat both meat and plants, so they are carnivorous and herbivorous (hər biv´ər əs) They are also oviparous.

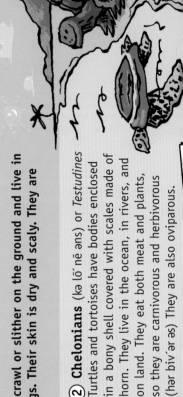

Galapagos tortoise

star tortoise

Their bodies have bony plates covered with scales. They are oviparous and lay eggs with hard shells that the young must break. They are carnivorous. There are 3 families:

Gavials, have a very long snout, live in India.

Alligators, have a wide snout, live in mild climates.

Crocodiles, have a thick neck and triangular snout, live in tropical areas.

④ Squamata

Covered with scales, they include Serpentes (snakes) and Sauria (lizards).

Serpentes

Over 2,800 species

Snakes have elongated bodies and no legs. They are carnivorous. They are oviparous or **ovoviviparous.*** There are many types of snakes, including boas, pythons, vipers and cobras.

> ***Ovoviviparous**
> (ō´vō vīp´ər əs):
> young develop in eggs that remain inside the mother's body until they hatch and are then born live.

green python

snake

cobra

viper

Sauria

About 3,800 species

Almost all *lizards* have four well-developed legs that lift their bodies off the ground. Most are oviparous, some ovoviviparous.

- Most lizards are insectivores, but some are carnivores (flying dragon, collared lizard, Komodo dragon, slow worm...) or herbivores.

flying dragon

frilled lizard

slow worm

monitor lizard

- Geckos can walk upside down.

- Chameleons are insectivores.

19

The frog's eggs float on the surface of the water.

The tadpole is born with a long tail for swimming and with gills for breathing under water.

Little by little, the gills are replaced by lungs and the back legs begin to appear.

At 12 weeks, the eyes begin to protrude and the mouth widens. The tail disappears and the front legs develop.

When the back legs are well formed, the frog jumps onto land. Its lungs fill with air.

What Is an Amphibian?

Amphibians lead double lives. Most of them are born and undergo metamorphosis in water, but they then live mostly on land as adults. One example is the frog.

The skin of most amphibians is smooth and moist. Sometimes it has glands that produce a sticky coating; other glands may produce poison.

Unlike the skeletons of salamanders, most frogs have a short spinal column, very short ribs, and no tail.

Anura, including frogs, have squat bodies. The bodies of urodeles, which includes salamanders, are elongated, allowing them to crawl. Apoda have neither legs nor fins.

Frogs are oviparous and abandon their eggs in the water. Most salamanders are ovoviparous: the eggs develop and hatch in the body of the mother and the babies are born live.

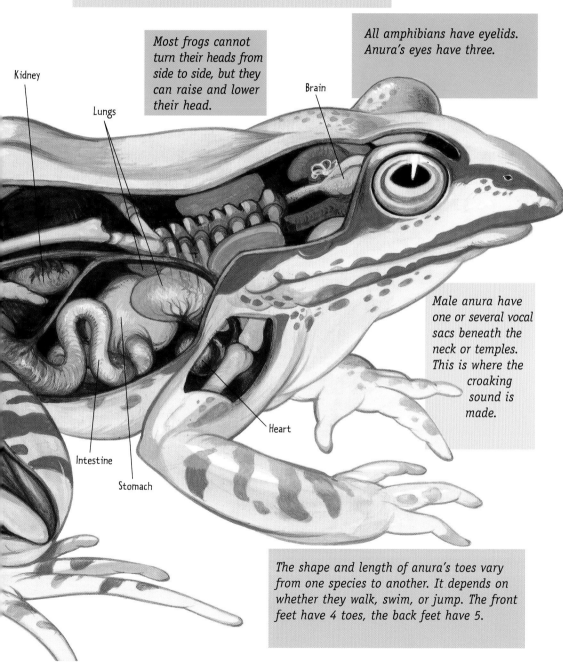

There are several different ways amphibians can breathe:
— through the gills or lungs
— through the skin if it is moist
— through the mouth, which the animal fills with air (anura) or water (urodele).

Most frogs cannot turn their heads from side to side, but they can raise and lower their head.

All amphibians have eyelids. Anura's eyes have three.

Male anura have one or several vocal sacs beneath the neck or temples. This is where the croaking sound is made.

The shape and length of anura's toes vary from one species to another. It depends on whether they walk, swim, or jump. The front feet have 4 toes, the back feet have 5.

Kidney

Lungs

Brain

Heart

Intestine

Stomach

What Is a Reptile?

With or without legs, all reptiles are able to slither or crawl. One type of reptile is a rattlesnake.

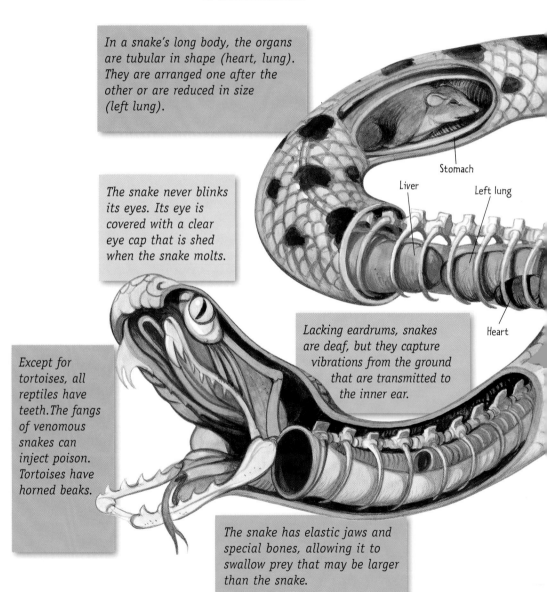

In a snake's long body, the organs are tubular in shape (heart, lung). They are arranged one after the other or are reduced in size (left lung).

The snake never blinks its eyes. Its eye is covered with a clear eye cap that is shed when the snake molts.

Except for tortoises, all reptiles have teeth. The fangs of venomous snakes can inject poison. Tortoises have horned beaks.

Lacking eardrums, snakes are deaf, but they capture vibrations from the ground that are transmitted to the inner ear.

The snake has elastic jaws and special bones, allowing it to swallow prey that may be larger than the snake.

Stomach

Liver

Left lung

Heart

Oviparous reptiles (such as turtles and crocodiles) bury their eggs in a warm pit in the ground. Certain pythons and cobras incubate them by covering them with their bodies. Ovoviparous lizards and snakes incubate the eggs inside their bodies.

Reptiles have skin covered with scales. A tortoise's body is protected by a bony shell covered with horned plates. Crocodilians have bony plates on their bodies.

Kidney

Intestine

The number of vertebrae a reptile has can vary a lot: at least 200 for a snake, 26 for a crocodile, 20 for a turtle.

Turtles, crocodiles and lizards move on four legs, except for the slow worm, whose limbs have disappeared. Snakes have no limbs.

When a rattlesnake shakes its tail, it makes a "rattling" sound that may frighten off its enemies.

■ How a royal python molts

When it feels its skin is too tight, the python molts to get rid of the top layer of skin. It may molt several times a year depending on its size and age.

The full molting process lasts 6 to 10 days. First the snake's skin grows soft.

Its eyes become veiled with a bluish white covering. The snake cannot see as well. It becomes irritable.

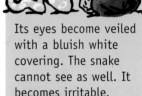

The molting itself takes 1 to 2 hours. It begins at the head. The old skin breaks off from the lips and eyes, then turns inside out like a glove all along the body to the end of the tail.

Cold-blooded Animals

Unlike mammals and birds, amphibians and reptiles are cold-blooded animals. They regulate their temperature by taking advantage of their environment.

1 *At night, the desert is frigid. The lizard buries itself in a lair that is 60° F. Its body temperature is 62.5° F.*

2 *In the early morning, the temperature is cool. The lizard warms itself in the sun on a rock. Its temperature can rise to 86° F in less than half an hour.*

■ A day in the life of a lizard

A lizard seeks the right temperature by changing place and posture. It warms up by exposing itself to the sun to gather energy so it can hunt. But it is quick to seek shade when the temperature gets too high: this keeps its body from overheating.

■ Controlling its temperature

An iguana's skin changes color according to the temperature. In the early morning and late afternoon its skin is dark, to absorb the heat. In the hotter times of day, its skin is light, reflecting the sun's rays.

3 *At mid-morning, the sun shines brightly. The lizard's dark skin absorbs the solar heat. Its temperature stabilizes at 95° F. It hunts insects and flees from predators.*

4 *At noon, the temperature nears 120° F. The lizard stays in the shade.*

5 *In the afternoon, when the temperature drops, it "lounges" in the sun or on warm rocks to maintain its 95° F body heat. It digests during this time.*

6 *When the sun goes down, the lizard returns to its lair.*

The squirming lizard

To walk on burning hot sand, the lizard does acrobatics. It lifts up its left front and right rear feet at the same time, allowing them to cool off. Then it walks a little more and pauses again to cool the other two feet.

Recharging its batteries

To be active, reptiles must have energy. One way to get energy is to warm themselves by basking in the sun.

Daily Life

People often feel repulsed by amphibians. Yet they are animals with amazing abilities!

■ How do frogs orient themselves?

A group of frogs was accustomed to laying eggs in a certain pond. One day, workers filled it in and created a road. Entirely new smells spread through the area. Yet the following year, the amphibians came right back to the same spot . . . because they orient themselves by the sun, not by scent.

■ Record jumps

Not all frogs jump. Some swim, others walk, soar, or climb trees. Frogs that live in trees are impressive acrobats. Tree frogs that are only 1.2 inches long can sometimes jump two feet. Rocket frogs can jump up to 15 feet!

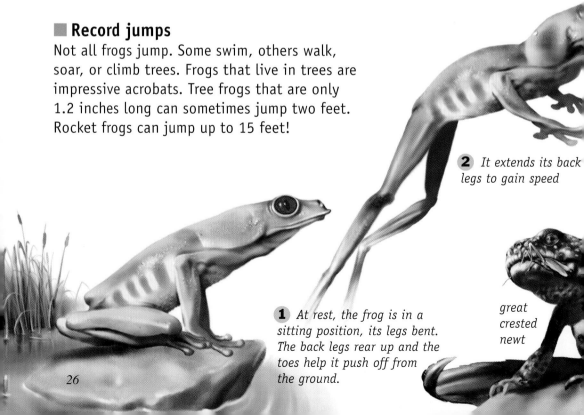

2 *It extends its back legs to gain speed*

great crested newt

1 *At rest, the frog is in a sitting position, its legs bent. The back legs rear up and the toes help it push off from the ground.*

■ Beware: poison!

Poison dart frogs manufacture strong venom in tiny glands on their backs. The poison is not fatal to the touch. However, if the poison gets into a body through the mouth or a wound, the victim can be quickly paralyzed and die. South American natives used the poison in frogs like these to poison their darts. Other amphibians also produce poisons. The European spotted salamander secretes poison into the mouth of a predator, so the animal will release it. The poison in these animals is the way they protect themselves. Predators learn to leave them alone!

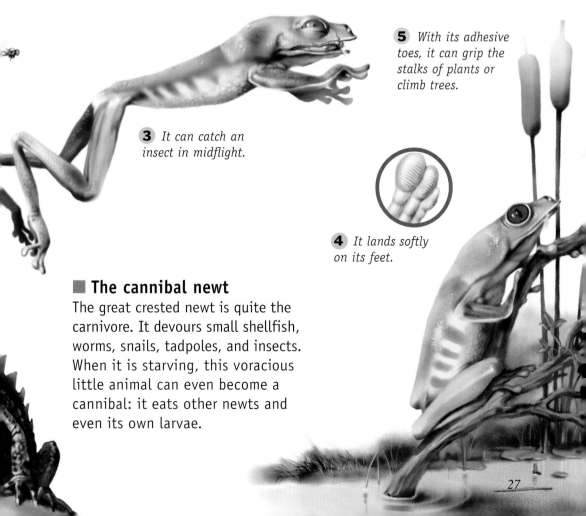

5 *With its adhesive toes, it can grip the stalks of plants or climb trees.*

3 *It can catch an insect in midflight.*

4 *It lands softly on its feet.*

■ The cannibal newt

The great crested newt is quite the carnivore. It devours small shellfish, worms, snails, tadpoles, and insects. When it is starving, this voracious little animal can even become a cannibal: it eats other newts and even its own larvae.

Seeing, Hearing, Touching

Depending on their needs and where they live, reptiles use their senses in many ways.

■ Snakes have no ears.

How does a snake learn about the world without ears? It is very sensitive to vibrations in the ground as it slithers along. With a long forked tongue that it flicks out, it can sense the odors of plants and animals. Its large eyes, covered with a transparent protective film, are always on the watch.

■ The mighty crocodile

The crocodile floats near the surface of the river. Leaving only the top of its skull above water, it smells and hears everything around it. Nostrils are located at the very end of its snout to detect odors. It lies in wait to surprise its prey—then grabs and drowns the prey in the water.

■ Hunting with infrared

Like many snakes, the pit viper is able to hunt at night. In total darkness, it can "see" using little cavities situated on each side of its head between the eyes and nostrils. These cavities can detect the heat or infrared radiation of a warm-blooded rodent. As soon as the prey moves, the viper attacks and injects its venom. Some-times the rodent escapes, but the snake will soon find it again by the heat the rodent gives off.

The Turtle or the Egg—Which comes first?

It is always the same: combat between rivals, attracting a female, and egg-laying.

Hermann's tortoises in the heat of combat

▪ Shell-to-shell combat

Two male turtles face off in front of the female, who stays on the sidelines. They rush at each other with the strength of a tank. Their shells strike and scrape each other. After two hours of intense fighting, one of them loses his balance. The other takes advantage of this and turns him over on his back, legs in the air. The victor leaves with the female he has won. The loser searches for a prop to turn himself back over again.

■ Eggs-actly!

In April, female ringed snakes take their first sunbath. They display their colored "necklaces" in the company of several males. One of them grows bold and approaches a female. In May, the males go away. In July, the females lay soft eggs, stuck together, beneath the grass. They hatch in September.

■ The leatherback sea turtle

The leatherback sea turtle goes ashore to lay her eggs. She digs a hole in the sand, where she lays 60 to 100 eggs. When she has finished, she is exhausted. She covers the eggs to hide them. Then she returns to the sea, sweeping the sand with her back feet to cover any trace of her presence so that predators do not know where the eggs are.

Family Life of the Crocodile

Before a Nile crocodile can attract a female, he must eliminate his rival!

Two adult males become aggressive rivals at the start of the courting season.

They arch their necks, wave their tails, slap the water, then plunge their heads in the river and spout water out of their nostrils.

The stronger one keeps up the pressure until the weaker one exposes his throat. Then the winner seizes the loser's foot in his jaws.

To attract a female, the crocodile follows a strict ritual.

Male and female lift their heads at the same time, then rub snouts.

Then they open their mouths wide without biting or harming each other.

The defeated one flees, swimming rapidly away.

The female returns faithfully each year to the same nest.

Using her back legs, she digs a hole about 15 inches deep.

She hunts nearby and prevents intruders and any other females from approaching.

She lays 15 to 80 eggs and does not eat during the three months that the eggs incubate.

All the males patrol the area.

The eggs are about to hatch.

Inside the shell, the tiny crocodiles begin to cry out. They can be heard from 60 feet away!

The female returns to the nest and rakes the soil with her jaws and forefeet to dig out the eggs.

Each hatchling breaks its shell with a tooth on the end of its snout. At last it comes out into the air.

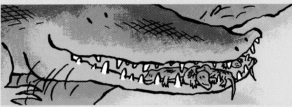

The mother cups her tongue to cradle her wriggling babies. Some have already wandered away and are giving out anxious calls. She collects all of them in her mouth and goes to the river.

For several weeks, the parents protect the nest together.

She shakes her head to deposit them in the water. The young swim around for awhile, then return to land, crying.

If a baby gives a sharp distress cry, all of them take shelter in the grass or hide in the water.

The young work together to dig tunnels up to 10 feet long.

Inside this shelter, 4 or 5 of the young are well protected . . .

. . . from countless predators: herons, storks, hyenas, crabs, large fish, and even other reptiles.

■ Swallowing an egg in its shell

The egg-eater snake (Dasypeltis) ingests huge eggs, shell and all. Thanks to its elastic jaws, it avoids breaking them.

When it has completely swallowed the egg, a bony saw in its esophagus* slices the egg apart.

The contents of the egg are released into the stomach. Delicious!

The reptile then spits out the pieces of shell.

Esophagus:
(ĭ sof´e gəs) Digestive canal leading from the mouth to the stomach.

What's on the Menu

Snakes and crocodiles are carnivores. Lizards are insectivores, but some are also carnivores or herbivores (hur´bə vors). Most land turtles eat plants, while sea turtles live on crabs, jellyfish, fish, and algae.

■ Thirst quenching cactus

In the dry season, a giant tortoise might quench its thirst by drinking the water inside big cactus plants. It tears off a piece, which falls to the ground. The tortoise breaks it open and swallows the pulp inside. In the rainy season, the tortoise drinks its fill from ponds.

A sweet tooth for jellyfish

When the leatherback sea turtle fills its lungs with air, it can dive nearly 1,000 feet deep in the sea. There it feasts on jellyfish. It can hold its breath for 20 to 30 minutes. After it comes back to the surface to breathe, it plunges back down to the depths. Some sea turtles have mistaken a plastic bag for a jellyfish and strangled to death.

Boa devouring a gazelle

Boa eats boa

The boa constrictor takes up a post in a tree to watch for prey. This powerful snake from the tropics wraps its body around the mammal and crushes it before eating it. Its mouth stretches to swallow the animal, alive or dead. When it has fully ingested the prey, its scales spread apart. Its body relaxes. As the boa digests, it remains motionless for weeks or months.

Another type of boa is the anaconda. If two anaconda snakes grab hold of the same prey, the larger snake may simply swallow the smaller snake.

Looking for Prey

**Crocodiles, snakes, lizards . . .
each reptile has its special
hunting technique!**

■ The ferocious
Komodo dragon

This large monitor lizard smells by using its bifurcated*
tongue to sample the air. With its keen sense of smell,
it can detect prey up to 1000 feet away. A bite from
this reptile is usually fatal, due to deadly bacteria in
its saliva. After biting its prey, the Komodo dragon can
simply follow until the animal falls or dies. In one
meal it can eat 80% of its body weight (a 10-foot
Komodo dragon weighs 350 pounds).

Bifurcated : (bī´ fər kāt´əd) Split into two parts, forked.

36

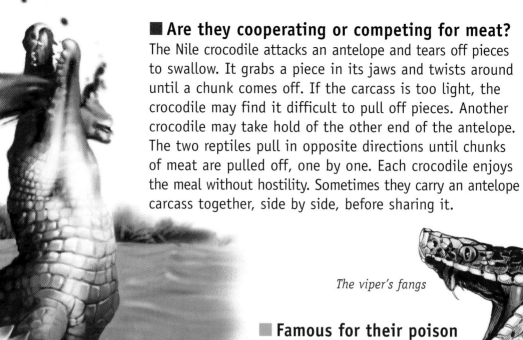

■ Are they cooperating or competing for meat?

The Nile crocodile attacks an antelope and tears off pieces to swallow. It grabs a piece in its jaws and twists around until a chunk comes off. If the carcass is too light, the crocodile may find it difficult to pull off pieces. Another crocodile may take hold of the other end of the antelope. The two reptiles pull in opposite directions until chunks of meat are pulled off, one by one. Each crocodile enjoys the meal without hostility. Sometimes they carry an antelope carcass together, side by side, before sharing it.

The viper's fangs

■ Famous for their poison

In its jaw, the pit viper has a pair of hollow, needle-like fangs invisible from the outside. A venom gland is situated at the base of the fangs. When the snake strikes, it expels the poison through the fangs, injecting it into the prey. The prey goes into shock and dies.

Secretion :
(sĭ krē´shən)
A substance produced by the body.

The Gila monster, a venomous lizard of Arizona, also has a venom gland, but its secretions* mix directly with its saliva. This helps it to defend itself and to prey on small mammals and other reptiles.

Gila monster

Protection From Predators

Turtles, snakes, lizards . . . different reptiles have different ways of escaping their enemies.

◼ A protective shell

The turtle has a shell that surrounds and protects it. The shell is formed of bony plates that are joined beneath its belly. When danger appears, the turtle retracts its four legs, head, and short tail into this hard, solid shelter. Young turtles, however, are very vulnerable because their shells are still soft.

◼ Hiss

Snakes "hiss" in different ways. The sand viper rubs its coarse scales together and produces a vibrating raspy sound. When the rattlesnake shakes its tail vigorously, it can be heard over 30 feet away. The bull snake has a very loud hiss. A flap within its larynx* vibrates, amplifying the hiss when it expels air.

> *****Larynx** :(lar´ ingks) Part of the inner throat that contains the vocal chords.*

Rattlesnake

Sand viper

Bull snake

■ Play dead

When a predator approaches, a hognose snake will squirm, stretch, hiss, and pant to try to scare it off. But if the enemy persists, the hognose changes strategy. It plays dead, going stiff and motionless with its mouth open and its tongue hanging out. It seems to stop breathing. It even emits a smell of death.

Attacked by a raccoon, a Blanding's turtle huddles in its shell.

■ Lose a tail

When a bird of prey goes after a skink in the Australian desert, the reptile will break off its own tail to escape. The tail falls off, but grows back fairly quickly. The second tail is shorter and lighter in color than the first.

Strange Lizards

There are about 3,800 lizard species on the planet. Some of them are really amazing!

Scare your enemies

The frilled lizard, which lives in Australia and New Zealand, averages 33 inches in length. In its neck it hides a fold of skin that can lie flat or flare out into a wide collar. It flips it out suddenly, opens its mouth wide, and hisses to intimidate and drive off an attacker. It's all a bluff! Despite all the fanfare, the lizard has no real defenses.

Walk on water

The basilisk lives in the marshlands of Central America. It swims, dives, or holds perfectly still in the middle of the swamp to avoid a predator. But it is also able to run across the surface of the water, on two legs and with toes splayed, as adeptly as on land. It can run across the water at nearly 7 1/2 miles per hour, fast enough to keep it from sinking.

Which end is which??

The worm lizard looks like a blind snake. This odd reptile seems to have a head at both ends, but one is really a tail. A lizard without legs, it moves backward as easily as forward, like an earthworm. With its snout it digs underground tunnels as its home.

Little dinosaur

Moloch horridus, nicknamed the "thorny devil," lives in the desert of central Australia. This frightening lizard has huge thorns on its head, body, and limbs. When threatened, it buries its face between its legs. All the attacker sees are the bristling horns on its head. Although it looks like a scary dinosaur, the moloch is only about 8 inches long and eats only ants all year round.

It changes color

The skin of a chameleon can change color. Many scientists believe that for some types of chameleons, what they are feeling can affect the color of their skin. They become green if they are content, gray if they are in pain, or black if they are angry. When a chameleon's skin changes to brown, it can warm up better by taking in sun rays. Some of the colors, such as brown or green, can also help the chameleon blend into the colors of trees and help it hide from predators.

It makes a "big" impression

When an enemy appears, the chameleon puffs up its body. Its lungs and several inflatable sacs in its belly fill with air. Then it opens its mouth and rocks back and forth threateningly. When the danger has passed, it deflates.

To move about, the chameleon clings tightly with its feet and moves them very carefully, one at a time. Its five toes act like pliers to grip a branch.

Its tail locks onto the branch and wraps around it to steady the lizard.

The Magic Chameleon

To survive in a hostile world, the chameleon has several ways to make up for its weaknesses.

■ It sticks out its tongue!

At rest, a chameleon's tongue folds up like an accordion. When it sees a grasshopper, its muscles activate with dazzling speed. The elastic tongue stretches to become as long as its body. With perfect accuracy, it captures the prey on its sticky tip. The lizard draws the insect back to its mouth, where its gummy lips grab and devour it.

◻ It crosses its eyes!

The chameleon is a strange hunter. Very patient, it waits for hours to spot prey. Its eyes can move independently of each other and are ringed with a large protective eyelid.

1 *With one eye, it explores the terrain and zeroes in on approaching insects.*

2 *With the other, it watches the spot where the insect will land. It attacks insects only when they are still.*

3 *The two eyes converge on its prey: its tongue darts out.*

Puzzle

Panic in the vivarium!

In this scene, the illustrator was supposed to show only reptiles and amphibians escaping from a vivarium (vī var´ē əm). But he couldn't resist the temptation to throw in a few other animals: mammals, birds, fish, insects. Can you find the 20 intruders? (If you are only borrowing this book, please do not make any marks on the page, so the next reader can have fun with this too!) Solution on page 49

Tricky Maneuvers

In every aspect of life, reptiles show their shrewdness. Some of the things they do . . .

Snakes that live in underbrush have intricate, interwoven designs.

■ Pretend to be female

When the male garter snake of Canada emerges from eight months of hibernation, it "disguises" itself as a female. How? It gives off the **pheromones*** of the opposite sex. The trickster attracts a swarm of other males (a hundred or so) who emerged before he did. They form a teeming ball around him, which warms him and helps him to revive. This also protects the still drowsy snake from predatory birds.

*Pheromone: (fer´ə mōn) Substance secreted by an animal that causes certain reactions in another animal of the same species.

■ Fly like a dragon

Flying dragons (Draco volans) have "wings" formed by ribs and membranes that extend out from each side of their body. At rest, these membranes lie alongside the body. When in danger, the dragon opens them like a parachute and drops away. They can glide 65 feet from tree to tree. When they land, their "wings" fold back in.

Those that live in trees are often slim and willowy, with green or brown colors.

■ Use camouflage
To blend in with its surroundings, snakes wear camouflage.

Some harmless species escape from their enemies because they look like venomous snakes . . .

Those that live in sandy deserts are yellow, beige, or light brown.

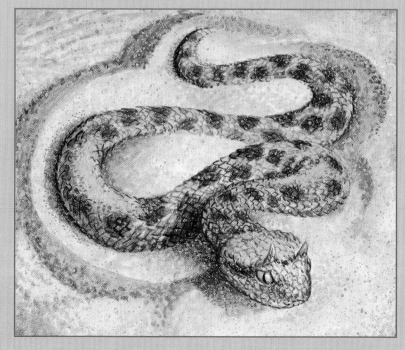

Incredible, but True!

A Lizard that Squirts Blood

A horned lizard (also called a horned toad) has a very bizarre defense against predators. It can burst tiny blood vessels around its eyes, then squirt out a three-foot jet of blood. Eeew! Shivers guaranteed.

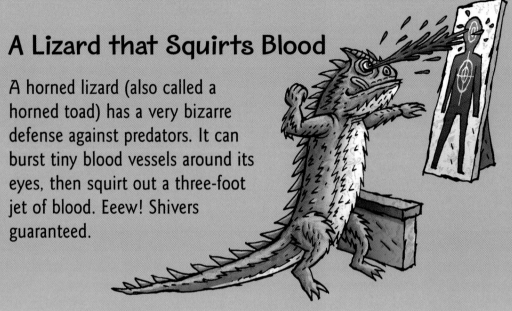

Is It a Boy or a Girl?

In some species of reptiles and amphibians, newborns may be more likely to be male or female, depending upon the temperature of the eggs as they incubate. One example is the Australian water skink. If the eggs are incubated at 90 degrees Fahrenheit, the newborns will all be males. At 86 degrees Fahrenheit, only 75% will be males.

Answers to the puzzle on pages 44-45

The following are neither a reptile nor an amphibian!

From top to bottom and left to right:
Bat, giraffe, pterodactyl, fish, pig, penguin, fox, sea anemone, marmoset, hedgehog, sea scallop, lobster, snail, seahorse, butterfly, starfish, rat, dung beetle, crab, spider.

Did You Know?

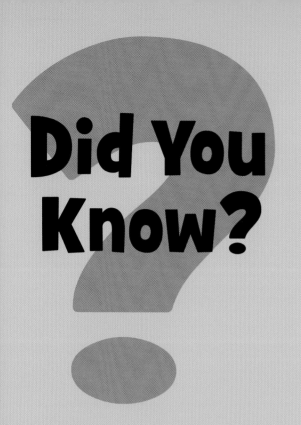

→ **How many times can a crocodile lose its teeth?**

Twice?
Ten times?
More than 20 times?

Its teeth can fall out more than 20 times and be replaced by new, fully developed ones.

→ **How does the pit viper find prey?**

It smells it?
It hears it?
It detects its body heat?

The pit viper hunts by sensing infrared rays from an animal's body heat.

→ **How does the skink defend itself from a vulture?**

It plays dead?
It loses its tail?
It runs away?

It can try to run away, but it can also lose its tail, which will grow back.

→ **Why is the midwife toad called by that name?**

Because it helps the female lay her eggs?

Because it carries the eggs for several weeks?

The males carry the eggs for several weeks.

→ **Where does a snake's molting start?**

At the head?

At the tail?

At a rip in the old skin?

At the head. The skin then peels off like a glove.

→ **What kind of reptile is a Komodo "dragon"?**

An iguana?

A monitor lizard?

A basilisk?

100% pure dragon

A monitor lizard. (And this dragon cannot breathe fire!)

→ **What is so strange about the horned lizard?**

Its eyes have no lids, so it licks them to moisten them?

Its eyes can squirt jets of blood?

Its eyes pivot so it can see in two directions at once?

Its eyes can squirt jets of blood.

A "Boa" Scarf

You can use old socks to make yourself a colorful "boa" scarf. .... Just be sure to get permission and help from your parents!

You'll need:
Your parent's help and permission
- **8** worn-out (but washed!) socks of different colors
- **1** pair of scissors
- **1** spool of thread
- **1** thick upholstery needle with rounded point
- **4** buttons
- **1** felt-tip pen
- **1** small square of yellow or orange felt
- **10** feet of rickrack (green, orange, purple ...)
- white glue

1 Set aside two socks with toes intact. They will become the head and tail of the snake. Cut them off before the curve of the heel. Cut the six other socks into two tubes each.

2 Use the pen to draw the shape of the tongue on the felt. Cut it out with the scissors and glue it onto the end of the sock that will be the snake's head.

3 For the body, put two tubes together end to end, slightly overlapping. Thread the needle with about 12 inches of thread, knot the end, and have an adult help you to sew (or show you how to sew) the two tubes together. When you are done, make another knot and cut off the end of the thread.

4 Put the rest of the tubes together in the same way, finishing up with the head and the tail. Cut 14 lengths of rickrack about 8 inches long. Put glue on one of the lengths and paste it onto the seam between two tubes to hide the stitches. Glue on the rest in the same way.

5 For the eyes, thread the needle with 8 inches of thread and knot the end. Sew a large button onto the boa's head, poking the needle through the button's holes. Sew the small button onto the large one, make another knot, and cut off the end of the thread. Make the second eye in the same way.

If you liked **Reptiles and Amphibians,**
here is another Half and Half™ book you are sure to enjoy!

Giants of the Ocean

STORY: In the story, a young girl is drifting on a raft in the middle of the ocean. Circling the raft is a huge shark, just waiting for a wave to knock the girl into the sea. Suddenly, a dolphin appears . . . and what happens next will amaze you!

HALF and **HALF**

Giants of the Ocean

GREAT STORY & COOL FACTS

LEVEL 3

FACTS: After the story, the book is packed with exciting information! Did you know there is a whale with a long twisted horn like a unicorn? Did you know there are crocodiles that swim in the ocean? You'll learn about animals of the ocean that are endangered— and some of the things that are being done to help protect them. Plus, find out how killer whales catch seals, how dolphins sleep, and much more!

To see all the Half and Half books that are available, just go online to **www.HalfAndHalfBooks.com**